DISCARD

China and Mao Zedong

Jack Dunster

Published in cooperation with Cambridge University Press
Lerner Publications Company, Minneapolis

Spelling of Chinese names

It is not easy to turn Chinese names into the sounds of the English alphabet, and there are two main ways of doing it. The older is called the Wade-Giles system (Pekin, Shensi, Mao Tse-tung), but now Pinyin is more usual (Beijing, Shaanxi, Mao Zedong) because it is closer to the Chinese sounds. This book uses Pinyin, and the alternative spellings are given at the back. A 'c' in Pinyin is pronounced 'ts', and 'x' is 'sh', so try saying the name of the Empress Ci Xi with these sounds.

LIBRARY OF CONGRESS CATALOGING IN PUBLICATION DATA

Dunster, Jack.
   China and Mao Zedong.

   (A Cambridge topic book)
   Originally published: Mao Zedong and China.
   Includes index.
   Summary: Traces the life and career of the Chinese peasant who rose to become chairman of the People's Republic during the turbulent period of China's revolution and transformation.
   1. Mao, Tse-tung, 1893-1976. 2. Heads of state— China—Biography. 3. China—History—Republic, 1912-1949. 4. China—History—1949-   . [1. Mao, Tse-tung, 1893-1976. 2. Heads of state. 3. China—History —20th century] I. Title.
DS778.M3D86   1983   951.05'092'4 [B] [92]   83-1854
ISBN 0-8225-1230-0 (lib. bdg.)

This edition first published 1983 by Lerner Publications Company
by permission of Cambridge University Press.

Original edition copyright © 1982 by Cambridge University Press
part of *The Cambridge Introduction to the History of Mankind: Topic Book*
under the title *Mao Zedong and China.*

International Standard Book Number: 0-8225-1230-0
Library of Congress Catalog Card Number: 83-1854

Manufactured in the United States of America

This edition is available exclusively from:
Lerner Publications Company, 241 First Avenue North, Minneapolis, Minnesota 55401

1 2 3 4 5 6 7 8 9 10 92 91 90 89 88 87 86 85 84 83

Contents

Introduction

MAO ZEDONG (1893-1976) was born of hard-working peasants in a small village, but he rose to establish the People's Republic of China. His story runs parallel with that of China's revolution and transformation. In the restless first half of the twentieth century Mao and his country each sought independence, sought to escape from poverty, ignorance and obsolete tradition. He adapted communism to apply it to the rural majority of the population. Many people were killed and liberties were restricted, but he restored the health and livelihood of the peasants and workers. China regained her world place as a powerful independent nation.

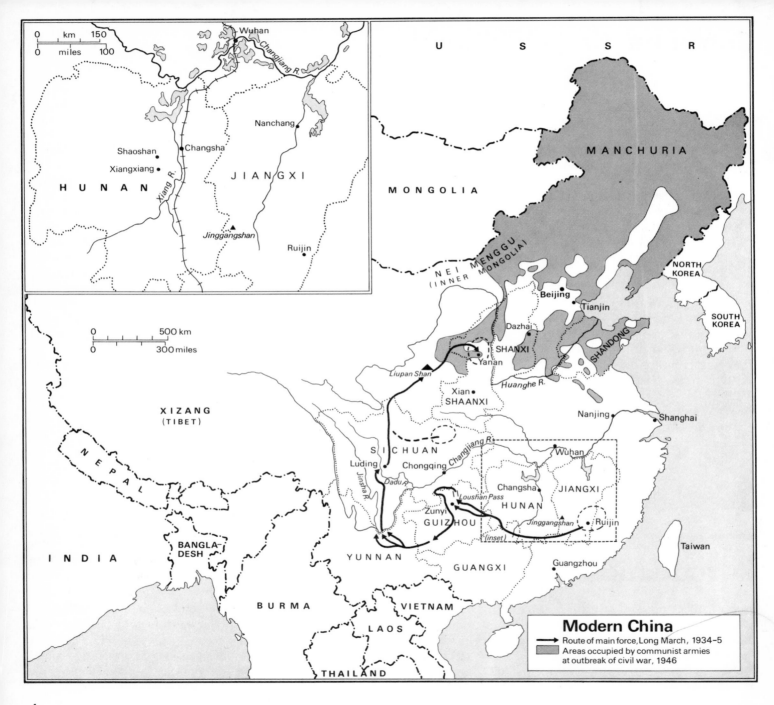

0 km 150
0 miles 100

Wuhan

Changjiang R.

Nanchang

Shaoshan
Xiangxiang
Changsha

Xiang R.

JIANGXI

HUNAN

Jinggangshan

Ruijin

U. S. S. R.

MANCHURIA

MONGOLIA

NEI MENGGU
(INNER MONGOLIA)

Beijing
Tianjin

NORTH
KOREA

SOUTH
KOREA

Dazhai

SHANXI
Yanan

SHANDONG

0 500 km
0 300 miles

Liupan Shan

Huanghe R.

XIZANG
(TIBET)

Xian
SHAANXI

Nanjing
Shanghai

NEPAL

SICHUAN

Changjiang R.

Wuhan

Luding
Chongqing

Jinsha R.
Dadu R.

JIANGXI

INDIA

BANGLA-
DESH

Loushan Pass
Zunyi
GUIZHOU

Changsha
HUNAN

Jinggangshan
(inset)
Ruijin

YUNNAN

Taiwan

GUANGXI

Guangzhou

BURMA

VIETNAM

LAOS

THAILAND

Modern China

→ Route of main force, Long March, 1934–5

▨ Areas occupied by communist armies
at outbreak of civil war, 1946

1   A questing childhood

Peasants of the Chinese empire

By the late nineteenth century the southern province of Hunan had a long-standing reputation for political disturbance and intellectual activity. The name Hunan means 'south of the lake', and the major thoroughfare for commercial traffic is the Xiang River, which flows north through the capital Changsha and on into a lake in the Changjiang River basin. In the village of Shaoshan hidden in a valley among steep, heavily wooded hills to the west of the Xiang River, Mao Zedong was born on 26 December 1893.

His father, then aged twenty-three, was a hard-working peasant of very little education. His mother, though illiterate, was gentle and understanding. In due course his parents had three more children, two younger sons, Zetan and Zemin, and an adopted daughter referred to as Zehong. Their cottage had walls of mud-bricks, a thatched roof and a floor of beaten earth. Nearby was a lotus pond in which the young Mao learned to swim. The climate of Hunan is sub-tropical.

As a small boy Mao had to work long and hard for his father on such jobs as weeding, bean-picking and rice-planting. After starting school at the age of seven he continued to work in the fields early each morning and late into the evenings. At the Nam An primary school he had to learn the Chinese classics by heart and, as he recalled later, it was there that he experienced his first successful rebellion. He stubbornly refused to stand and recite his lessons, arguing that he could do so equally well while seated. No doubt both his teacher and his father found him an unusually difficult child.

Like all Chinese fathers, Mao's expected total obedience. He was also determined to work and save enough to buy land of his own rather than go on paying heavy rent to a landlord. By 1903 he owned a small farm. But though his prosperity and his importance in the village were growing, he faced difficulties with his son. Young Mao Zedong, like many Chinese of his generation, questioned the old traditions of respect for their elders.

In 1906 Mao was withdrawn from school to help full-time on his father's expanding property. He did not particularly resent this move, but two years later he rebelled strongly. Following one of the traditions of which Mao most disapproved, his father arranged that he marry a girl four years his elder. Mao stubbornly refused to have any contact with her. The marriage of his mother, to whom he was devoted, had been similarly arranged, and he resented what he saw as her state of bondage. Decades later one of the first new laws he introduced as Chairman of the People's Republic was a Marriage Law based on monogamy (having only one husband or wife at a time) and freedom of choice.

While at school he had learned to read. At home he continued to read nightly by the light of a wick suspended in a pot of vegetable oil. Among his favourite novels were *Water Margin* (sometimes called *All Men are Brothers*) and *Romance of the Three Kingdoms*. The heroes of the first of these books were rebels who in bygone times devoted themselves to correcting injustice. He read both books repeatedly.

The troubles of the empire

From time to time young Mao had heard of war, and of dispute in the distant capital, the city of Beijing (which the British called Peking). In 1895 China suffered a humiliating defeat by Japan. But when, in 1898, the young Emperor and his scholarly friend Kang Youwei attempted to introduce reforms and modernise China, they were ruthlessly overruled by the powerful, old-fashioned Empress Dowager and her military aide, Yuan Shikai. In 1900 (the year when Mao started school) the Boxer Uprising swept through northern China. It started as a peasant revolt, but the Empress and her friends turned it against the foreign powers that dominated

China. Japan, the United States, Britain, Germany, France and the other powers joined to send an army that destroyed the Boxers. Thereafter even the proud old Empress Dowager had to accept the need for some reforms. Both the army and the schools were modernised.

In 1906 there was trouble nearer home. Famine struck Hunan province. Peasants and miners marched into Changsha to demand food and were cut down by the army of the military governor. Mao, aged twelve, heard of the incident and the memory remained with him. He said later, 'I felt that there with the rebels were ordinary people like my own family and I deeply resented the injustice of the treatment given them.'

Four years later famine returned. Hungry poor from the village seized a load of rice which Mao's father was sending for profitable sale in the city. Mao sided with the villagers against his father, yet it worried him that neither attitude could solve the basic problem of poverty. After further protest against his elders' tyranny and ignorance he left home to enroll in a modern school in the busy town of Xiangxiang. He was now aged sixteen.

School and the world beyond

Away from his native village Mao's outlook broadened greatly. The school catered mainly to the well-dressed sons of the wealthy, and at first Mao was mocked for his humble clothes and rural background. However, his academic progress was swift and brilliant, and his interest was awakened in the world at large and in current events in China. He read avidly about famous people of the past such as Robespierre and Napoleon, George Washington and Abraham Lincoln. He also learned that China's Empress Dowager and the young Emperor had both died two years previously in 1908. He read of and thought about the different proposals to improve people's social welfare and to rescue China from its decline. At first he applauded the writings of Kang Youwei, who advised having an elected parliament together with the monarchy. On the other hand the Western-educated Dr. Sun Yat-sen and his associate Wang Jingwei wanted to do away with emperors altogether and have a republic with a parliament and a president. Soon Mao was forming his own political ideas.

Dowager Empress Ci Xi (1835–1908) effectively held power in China for most of 1861–1908. The portrait shows her fabulous wealth. Her long finger nails show respect for tradition and expectation that everything will be done for her. She feared that modernisation would destroy the empire.

With a good report from the modern school at Xiangxiang Mao was readily admitted in the following year to the middle school in the provincial capital, Changsha. He made the journey by river steamer. In the city he developed his interest in current affairs, while at the same time he trained regularly to keep fit. Unusually tall for a southerner, he set himself an exercise programme to develop his muscles and his sense of self-discipline.

|  **Key events** | 1900 | Boxer Uprising: a violent attempt to end foreign interference, crushed by an international army. |
| | 1911 | 10 October (the Double Tenth): republican revolution began at Wuhan. |

left: *This Western painting of a Beijing street at about the turn of the century shows agitated public reaction against foreign interference in China's internal affairs.*

below: *Under Manchu rule all Chinese had to wear their hair in a plait, a 'pigtail', or be beheaded. By early this century the punishment was public humiliation, but Mao cut off his pigtail to show support for the republican rebels.*

The republican revolution

The year was 1911. On October 10 revolution broke out in the city of Wuhan on the Changjiang River. Though Dr Sun was overseas raising funds and Wang Jingwei was in prison, the revolutionaries supported their republican ideas. The revolution was ill-timed and inadequately planned, but the movement spread rapidly.

Mao read press reports of the uprising. So excited was he that he deliberately cut off his pigtail. The Manchu emperors, who had ruled China since 1644, had imposed the wearing of pigtails on all Chinese males. To remove them was symbolic of revolt and punishable by beheading. Mao persuaded other middle school students to follow his example, and he lopped off the pigtails of those too frightened to do it themselves.

Barely two weeks after its outbreak in Wuhan, the fighting spread to Changsha in Hunan, which was the native province of some of the revolutionary leaders. Mao had been eager to go to Wuhan, but now he saw skirmishes on the outskirts of Changsha itself between revolutionaries and the local Manchu garrisons. Promptly he left school and enlisted in the cause of Sun Yat-sen.

By the time Dr Sun returned from overseas, the armed struggle was over. The militarist Yuan Shikai, the dismissed favourite of the late Empress Dowager, was recalled by the imperial government to suppress the rebels. But Yuan was an ambitious man with flexible ideas of loyalty. Instead of crushing the republicans he negotiated to end the monarchy, provided he himself became first president of the new republic.

Mao spent about five months as a soldier, apparently with no chance to fight. During 1912, supposing the revolution was completed, he left the army. For a short time he went back to middle school, but was too restless to continue there and decided to study alone. Throughout the next half-year he spent long hours daily at the Hunan Provincial Library learning the history and geography of other countries and reading translations of works by such thinkers as Adam Smith, John Stuart Mill and Charles Darwin.

At the age of seventy-one Mao wrote that his decision in 1912 to seek knowledge independently had been one of the most important turning points in his development.

2 The first republic

Key people

Yuan Shikai, 1859–1916. A clever soldier but vain, ambitious and untrustworthy. He betrayed first the Emperor, then the empire, and finally the republic that made him its president.

Dr Sun Yat-sen, 1866–1925. Attended a Christian school in Honolulu and took his British medical degree in Hong Kong. Travelled widely to rally support for his republican movement. His goal was the 'Three Principles of the People', generally summarised as nationalism, democracy, people's livelihood.

Sun Yat-sen and Yuan Shikai

Mao Zedong left the army in 1912 because he thought the revolution was over; but his hopes and those of the republicans were soon dashed.

Sun Yat-sen's ultimate goal was to establish his 'Three Principles of the People'. He never clearly defined them, but just before his death friends compiled a text based on his past lectures. The first principle called for nationalism, to rid China of foreign interference; the second called for moves towards democracy, a republic whose rulers would all be elected; the third, termed people's livelihood, involved steps to share out land and wealth more evenly so that there would be food and education for all. Dr Sun was an idealist rather than a practical man, and differences in interpretation of his Three Principles led eventually to civil war.

On 1 January 1912 Dr Sun became nominal president of the new republic, but as arranged he resigned in favour of Yuan Shikai. However, Yuan neglected the republicans in the south and took his oath of office in the northern capital Beijing. There, by the end of 1912, he set up a national assembly with his personally chosen cabinet. Meanwhile in the southern capital, Nanjing, the republican leaders planned elections for a new government. They formed the Nationalist Party, or Guomindang (GMD), to spread Sun's principles.

In the 1913 elections the GMD defeated most of Yuan's supporters. But Yuan was not prepared to give up power. GMD leaders were assassinated, or driven into exile, or bribed. Sun Yat-sen was forced to flee to Japan. In November Yuan banned the GMD itself, expelled its members from parliament, and abolished provincial assemblies. Yuan had made himself sole dictator.

Chinese supporters of democracy felt bitter. On the other hand most of the people understood little of the intended reforms, and many of the richer folk who did thought that their wealth would be safer under Yuan. Western countries had quite expected the republican bid to fail. They generally favoured Yuan, for Sun's nationalist principles threatened their interests. Five major foreign powers (Britain, France, Germany, Russia, Japan) gave Yuan a large Reorganisation Loan in cash. As security for the loan Yuan gave the whole of China's revenue from railways and taxes on salt production, thus angering the republicans even more. He used part of the loan to pay off army officers he no longer needed and so, unwittingly, enabled them to become independent warlords with their own private armies.

The weakness of China

In 1914 war broke out in Europe. Japan promptly joined in on Britain's side against Germany and seized her Asian possessions, including territory in the Chinese province of Shandong. Japan was enjoying a wartime industrial boom and wanted permanent access to China's mineral resources. While other countries were preoccupied with war, Japan secretly presented Yuan Shikai with twenty-one demands. They included all Germany's previous rights in China, new concessions in south Manchuria and Inner Mongolia, and other privileges designed to bring weak China under Japanese influence. This blatant greed shocked the rest of the world. But Yuan was forced to accept most of the demands, fearing that otherwise Japan might aid such enemies as Sun Yat-sen against him.

Many people in China, especially the students and intellectuals, felt enraged and humiliated. Yuan Shikai had already announced his intention of being crowned as emperor, and he mistook the general upsurge of feeling against Japan as popular support for himself. But many recalled his previous betrayals of trust. Now even his own generals turned against him. The southwestern provinces formally declared themselves independent, and Tibet also broke away. In June 1916 Yuan Shikai died, leaving a struggle for power between his former officers.

China seemed to be falling apart, leaderless. But the reform of military training at the start of the century had produced well-trained and well-equipped soldiers. This gave great power to the generals, the warlords. They were selfish men, each running his own part of the country in his own interests. The central government at Beijing kept little power; its membership changed constantly. Foreign powers were willing to deal with whatever regime happened to be in control, provided their trading rights and similar interests remained unhindered. Sun Yat-sen tried to set up a new republican government at Guangzhou in the far south. It soon failed and he had to take refuge in the French part of Shanghai. China was weaker than ever.

Mao the student

Through these years of political turmoil Mao Zedong was back at Changsha as a student. One of the educational reforms at the start of the century had been the setting up of Provincial Normal Schools. Officially secondary schools, these were more like colleges or local universities. Mao enrolled at Changsha Normal School in 1913 to train as a teacher. While the power struggle went on between Yuan, Sun and the warlords, Mao was absorbed into the social and academic interests of alert students. His five years at the Normal School were extremely important to his development.

In 1915 he was elected secretary of the students' society. Among other activities this staged public demonstrations against Yuan Shikai's dictatorship, Japan's twenty-one demands, and the selfishness of warlords. Later Mao became president of the society. He also created the 'Association for Student Self-Government' to resist the old-fashioned rules and regulations of the school. By 1917 he commanded the student volunteer defence force; and still he kept up his physical training, particularly distance swimming.

In his studies, too, Mao maintained a distinguished record. He improved his literary style and he came to love and respect China's unique cultural heritage. In later years Mao remembered one of his teachers, Yang Changji, who taught ethics, as one of the few older men whom he sincerely respected. Yang had had a thorough old-fashioned Chinese education; but he had followed it with ten years of study in Japan and Europe to broaden his knowledge of the modern world.

He taught Mao to understand the ideas of Western civilisations as well as China's own. Mao learned that whereas the past should never be ignored, the future matters even more; a nation may best secure its future by stimulating the initiative, talent and energy of every individual.

Yang Changji prompted his students to read the radical magazine *New Youth*. *New Youth* was published by a group of professors at Beijing University, led by Chen Duxiu, Dean of the Faculty of Letters. Chen, like Yang, had recieved a classical education followed by some years of study overseas. Returning to China, he took part in the revolutionary upheavals of 1911 and 1913 before taking high office at the university. In *New Youth* he strongly attacked many of the old Chinese ways. He argued that realistic planning for the future mattered more than traditional respect for the ideas and conduct of the ancient philosopher Confucius. *New Youth* also broke with tradition by using the common language instead of elaborate literary forms of expression, so students from all over the country exchanged new ideas by writing for the paper. In April 1917 the magazine published an article by Mao on physical culture, stressing his belief that good health and strength of character would help save China from the foreigners.

The 'New Thought Tide', as this radical movement was called, was furthered by the large number of young men who sought wider experience abroad. Many went to Japan, as the most progressive of Asian countries. Others went to

Key events

1915	Twenty-one demands from Japan.
1916–28	The warlords ruled over much of China.
1917–21	New Thought Tide led to revival of GMD and founding of the Chinese Communist Party (1921)

Key people

Chen Duxiu, 1879–1942. From a mandarin family, educated in Japan and France. Adopted Western ideas, edited the radical *New Youth* magazine, and led the May Fourth Movement. In 1920 took up Russian communist principles, and was from 1921 to 1927 general secretary of the Chinese Communist Party. He was blamed for the failure of the 1927 uprisings, eventually expelled from the CCP, and later imprisoned by the nationalists.

left: *Overseas work-and-study. Thousands of young men returned from abroad determined to rid China of its old-fashioned restrictions. This cartoon by a Mexican artist distinguished between examples back from England, France and America, but shows all three to differ greatly from traditional Chinese appearance and attitude.*

America, which had used the money China had been forced to pay her after the Boxer Uprising to provide scholarships for Chinese students. Some visited Britain, but the greatest number spent a few years in France. Work-and-study schemes enabled more than 2,000 intelligent young Chinese students to pay their way through their studies, and to acquaint themselves with the principles of 'liberty, equality and fraternity'; in addition, by 1918, some 140,000 Chinese workers had been recruited by the allies for work in France. Both Zhou Enlai, who studied in France, and Zhu De who studied in Germany, later became close associates of Mao Zedong. Mao himself, as student president in Changsha, was involved in recruiting young men for the work-and-study scheme.

Early in 1918 he had a major part in establishing yet another radical student society. By this time his last links with home were breaking. He was much grieved by the death of his mother. Two years later his father died having, by

sheer hard work and shrewd dealing, succeeded in joining the 'rich peasant class' which Mao Zedong despised.

During 1918 Mao graduated from the Normal School as a teacher. His outlook now, like that of many young men throughout China, was wordly and modern. He was reasonably well read and interested in political matters, but in his own words he was 'seeking the way'. He decided to go to Beijing. Mao's teacher, Yang Changji, had just accepted a professorship at Beijing University, and his daughter, Yang Kaihui, whom Mao much admired, would be there too.

As a young man of rural peasant background from a distant province it must have been very exciting for him to be in an international capital with a chance of meeting the leading thinkers and writers of the new China. Thanks to Yang Changji he obtained a post as assistant in the University Library. It was poorly paid, but it enabled him to join student societies and therefore to attend lectures. Soon he was increasingly influenced by the Dean, Chen Duxiu.

3 A sense of national purpose

Key events

1917	Russian Revolution: communists seized power. Their success encouraged revolutionaries everywhere.
1919	May Fourth Movement: students and intellectuals protested at China's treatment by foreigners.
1921	Chinese Communist Party founded in Shanghai.

Key groups

Guomindang (GMD) The Nationalist People's Party, formed in 1912 and re-founded in 1921 to pursue the ideals of Sun Yat-sen.

Chinese Communist Party (CCP) founded in 1921 to spread the ideas that had triumphed in the Russian Revolution.

Comintern The Russian-dominated Communist International, set up in 1919 to spread world-wide revolution.

The May Fourth Movement

In 1918, while warlord troops ravaged the countryside and most of China's people struggled to make a living, staff and students at Beijing University became increasingly concerned about China's danger from foreign interference. In particular, Chen Duxiu and his colleagues feared Japanese ambitions, shown in the twenty-one demands.

Consequently, when the Versailles Peace Conference in 1919 upheld Japan's claims to take over Germany's rights and territories in China, the members of the university marched into the streets in a great demonstration. This started the 'May Fourth Movement'. Chen Duxiu and over a thousand of his followers were arrested, but this only made people throughout China aware of their protest. The new movement attracted many of those already aroused by the New Thought Tide, and it spread to the provinces. The peasants, the vast rural majority, were not yet involved; but workers and students in most cities and towns staged strikes and demonstrations of protest, and Chinese merchants refused to handle Japanese or other foreign goods.

Mao had returned to his home province, Hunan, before the May Fourth Movement began. When he heard news of it he organised similar demonstrations in Changsha and arranged discussions between merchants, students and workers. He also published his own radical magazine called *Xiang River Review*. His influence in the province increased in 1920 when he became director of the primary school section of the Normal School where he had trained as a teacher. This post enabled him to marry Yang Kaihui, daughter of his old teacher; and also to visit Chen Duxiu, now released, for long talks. From that time onwards Mao regarded himself as a communist.

The Chinese Communist Party

Many other young men inspired by the May Fourth Movement also chose their political creeds. Leaders such as Sun Yat-sen and Chen Duxiu each saw a new value in recruiting the young to support their respective causes. The outcome of the 1917 Russian Revolution stimulated interest, but did not prompt an immediate response in China. During the May Fourth Movement the Russian communists won favour by giving up their country's special privileges in China. They sought to spread their ideas to other countries through the *Comintern*, or Communist International. Many Chinese, striving to build a new framework for society, welcomed those ideas. Communist groups appeared in several cities, and communist youth leagues formed in many schools and colleges. Mao promptly organised such groups in Changsha.

In July 1921 about a dozen representatives from these scattered groups, including Mao, met in the French-controlled section of Shanghai. There they founded the Chinese Communist Party, the CCP, with Chen Duxiu as its first general secretary. The new party received financial assistance and much advice from Moscow's Comintern; but in the years ahead, under the influence of Mao, CCP policies differed increasingly from those of Russia.

The United Front

One demand of the May Fourth Movement was for China to oppose foreign interference. America, worried by post-war developments, called an international conference at Washington late in 1921. The Washington conference agreed that no country should interfere in China, either to take territory or to demand special trading rights. Japan was persuaded to give back to China the Shandong area she had taken from Germany. But there still remained a Japanese threat to Manchuria in the north, and the unequal rights already given to other powers, especially Britain and France.

In common with Chen Duxiu and many others, Sun Yat-sen was anxious to rid China of such foreign interference. Dr Sun wanted to see China an independent and free democratic republic. He set about rebuilding the GMD, which had been abolished by Yuan Shikai. But he lacked the organisation and finance he needed. Naturally, he got no help from the foreign powers, whose privileges he wanted to curtail; so, like the CCP, he accepted aid from the Comintern.

In return for their help the Russians insisted that GMD and CCP should form an alliance to work as a United Front. Dr Sun agreed, and the CCP members joined the Guomindang. But Dr Sun insisted that the alliance was not to be a coalition of the parties. Communists were admitted to the GMD as individuals. They kept their Communist Party membership as well, forming 'a bloc within a bloc'.

The first headquarters of this United Front was in Guangzhou. For Mao, politics now mattered far more than his school work. He resigned his post in Changsha and went south to Guangzhou. There he worked with Dr Sun's assistant, Wang Jingwei, to arrange co-operation between the two parties.

One purpose of the United Front was to prepare a combined army. This would march north to reunify China by freeing it from competing warlords and from foreign demands. Dr Sun had chosen a young military commander to lead the joint army. His name was Chiang Kai-shek.

Mao admired both Dr Sun's ideals and Chiang's revolutionary zeal. He was keen to co-operate with them. He was worried by Chen Duxiu's respect for Russian advice which, Mao thought, did not really apply to the situation in China. As a result the GMD and CCP each began to suspect Mao of unduly favouring the other. By the end of 1924 the strain of trying to satisfy both sides made him ill and he returned to Hunan.

Peasant revolution

While Chiang Kai-shek trained his new army in Guangzhou, Mao, in his home province, started to prepare for a different type of revolutionary struggle by organising a union of workers and peasants. It was to be more in line with the many peasant uprisings of China's long history. He suggested to the GMD leaders that they should form a Peasant Department, and they duly established an institute in Guangzhou to train peasants in rural leadership. Mao became increasingly convinced that any plan for a new China must actively involve the peasants. After all, they made up four-fifths of China's people. But because the successful Russian Revolution of 1917 had been carried out by industrial workers and intellectuals, the Comintern advice on which Chen Duxiu relied continued to ignore the peasants.

Mao returned to Guangzhou in October 1925, soon after the death of Sun Yat-sen, and he was placed in charge of the Peasant Institute. He rapidly expanded its activities. By mid-1926 about a million peasants in southern China were organised into associations sponsored by the GMD as Mao had suggested. Only then did the CCP start to set up its own Peasant Department. Mao went to Shanghai to help set it up, using leaders he had trained at the GMD Institute.

Then he went back once more to Hunan to find out how the peasant movement there was progressing. The situation there convinced him that:

'In a very short time, in China's central, southern and northern provinces, several hundred million peasants will rise like a mighty storm, like a hurricane; a force so swift and violent that no power, however great, will be able to hold it back. They will smash all the trammels that bind them and rush forward along the road to liberation. They will sweep all the imperialists, warlords, corrupt officials, local tyrants and evil gentry into their graves.'

Key events	1923	United Front of GMD and CCP.
	1925	Death of Sun Yat-sen. Chiang Kai-shek became principal leader of Guomindang.
	1927	Shanghai massacre: Chiang ended the United Front.

In an old rent collection courtyard in Sichuan a large display of lifesize models shows the harsh attitude of old-time landlords. For peasants work was hard, rents high and food scarce. Mao won peasant support by promising fairer treatment.

Peasants and workers united in the Autumn Harvest Uprisings, 1927. A Chinese artist painted this at the time of the Cultural Revolution, 1968.

Chiang Kai-shek turns against the communists

Mao's intention was to influence the CCP leader, Chen Duxiu, towards recognising the part the peasants could play in a revolution. But his views and ideas alarmed Chiang Kai-shek. In July, 1926 Chiang reaffirmed GMD–CCP solidarity. His army then marched northwards on its mission to free and reunify China and speedily reached the Changjiang River. He and many of his officers were worried by the growing communist strength. Soon, they feared, the communists might dominate the GMD. Both parties wanted China to be reunited and independent, but Chiang began to fear the communists' revolutionary ideas as a worse threat than warlords or foreigners. He removed CCP members from all positions of influence or authority within the army. Mao supposed that move was meant to press Moscow into giving more aid and he did not object.

One young communist so removed from the staff of the military academy in Guangzhou was Zhou Enlai. Nevertheless, Zhou still worked for the common revolutionary cause. When Chiang's army, purged of CCP officers, advanced down the Changjiang towards the great international port of Shanghai, Zhou arranged a rising of the city's workers to take over the areas controlled by foreigners. Greatly to Zhou's surprise the army spurned this help. Instead, Chiang's soldiers turned against their former allies. They massacred all known communists and the workers who supported them. Zhou himself narrowly managed to escape. The GMD–CCP unity which Dr Sun had managed to maintain was now shattered.

Chiang's attack on the communists swiftly extended into other provinces, including Hunan. Mao was forced to flee. But a few months later, on 1 August 1927 the communists struck back. At Nanchang, Zhou Enlai helped to organise an armed uprising, led by a general of the former United Front, Zhu De.

Soon after, the communist leaders deposed Chen Duxiu. They planned a series of attacks, called the Autumn Harvest Uprisings. But they wanted to direct these against various southern cities. Against his personal inclination, Mao accepted orders to lead an attempted capture of Changsha although many CCP supporters there were already killed or disbanded. The scheme failed. With the remnant of his army of workers and peasants Mao retreated to a mountain area named Jinggangshan.

In that precipitous refuge the ragged communist army endured such hazards as wolves and bitter cold. They survived by bartering with primitive villagers for supplies, and they recruited more peasants from surrounding areas. In April 1928 they were joined by Zhu De with survivors from another unsuccessful CCP uprising. In November they were further reinforced by Peng Dehuai, a GMD officer who now changed sides bringing with him a large band of supporters. The men from these various sources were merged to form the Red Army, with Zhu De as military commander and Mao as political chief.

Encirclement

It might have seemed to Chiang Kai-shek that he had at last reunited China, save for the troublesome communists in a few scattered towns or country areas. In 1928 he took political as well as military control of the Guomindang. He became a Christian and married the sister of Sun Yat-sen's widow, daughter of a wealthy Shanghai merchant. These moves increased his political strength, enabling him to dismiss the Russians and receive instead American aid. His army cleared warlords – but not foreigners – from eastern and northern provinces. His government, based on Nanjing, was recognised internationally as ruling all China. He allowed foreigners to live and work as missionaries or merchants, but persuaded some Western governments to give up their territorial claims and, at least partly, to reduce duties they charged on goods of trade.

Chiang had one more avowed aim: he must wipe out the communists. He launched GMD assaults against Jinggang-shan. Mao and Zhu De realised that their refuge could neither protect them from such attacks nor provide for their needs throughout another winter. They had to move on. During the next couple of years from a new base in the wild border area of Jiangxi province, they again attacked cities such as Changsha and Nanchang as ordered by the CCP, but never with much success. In 1930 Mao's wife, Kaihui, and his sister, Zehong, were both captured and executed; their heads were displayed on spikes in Changsha as a warning to

any others who might support communists.

These disasters, following those of the Autumn Harvest Uprisings, convinced Mao that his party was waging war the wrong way. CCP leadership was still influenced by the Comintern, which advised revolution through urban workers and open conflict. In Mao's view the most urgent need was land reform, the most reliable force to achieve it was the peasantry, and the most effective form of warfare for their purpose was guerrilla tactics. He gained the peasants' support by encouraging them to take action against greedy landlords. He and Zhu De set up a *soviet*, or 'People's Republic' at Ruijin. The soviet grew rapidly in numbers and strength and controlled much of southern Jiangxi. By 1931 the CCP leaders, whose past meetings had been held secretly in Shanghai or Wuhan, also moved to Ruijin and took direct control. Zhu De still commanded the Red Army, but Zhou Enlai, recently returned from Moscow, took over from Mao as chief political officer.

The Jiangxi soviet posed a threat that Chiang Kai-shek determined to end. But his first three campaigns of annihilation, each stronger than the one before, were unsuccessful. Their failure was partly because peasants in surrounding areas misled the GMD armies and aided the communists, partly also because Zhu De's army adopted the sixteen-word guerrilla jingle which Mao wrote at this time:

'Enemy advances, we retreat;
enemy camps, we harass;
enemy tires, we attack;
enemy retreats, we pursue.'

Nevertheless Chiang's army was the better equipped and larger force. It should have won eventually were it not that in September 1931 Japan seized Manchuria. From then on Chiang's attention was divided between the threat of further Japanese invasion in the north and the menace of communist rebels in the south.

Chiang decided that the communists were the weaker and yet the more dangerous; his first priority was to destroy them. In 1933 his fifth campaign in Jiangxi also failed, but it left the soviet encircled by armed blockhouses. The communists were thus trapped in a narrow area; they were doomed to final destruction unless, once again, they moved on.

Key events		

Key events

1927 Autumn Harvest Uprisings: unsuccessful CCP attempts, based on Comintern advice, to seize cities in Hunan.

1928 The Red Army, later the People's Liberation Army, formed partly from mutinous GMD troops. Headed by Zhu De, it tried to keep friendly and helpful relations with all civilians.

1929 Jiangxi soviet set up by Mao and Zhu De.

1930–3 Chiang's five attempts to destroy the Jiangxi soviet, ending in encirclement.

1931 Japan seized Manchuria, created puppet state of Manchukuo.

Key people

Chiang Kai-shek, 1887–1975. Trained for the army in Japan, met Sun Yat-sen and accepted republican ideals. After GMD–CCP alliance, went to Russia for further training, then commanded Northern Expedition, 1926–8. Married sister of Sun's  widow, and became political as well as military leader, 'Generalissimo'. Won international recognition and financial aid for GMD government. Neglected land reform and social welfare. During war with Japan lost support because he seemed to prefer fighting communists. Defeated in civil war, he set up his regime in Taiwan.

Wang Jingwei, 1883–1944. Intellectual, close associate of Sun Yat-sen. Displaced by Chiang Kai-shek. Favouring a united East Asia, he urged peace with Japan, and later became head of Japan's 'puppet' government in occupied China.

Zhou Enlai, 1898–1976. From a gentry family, went to university in Japan, and work-and-study in France. Political worker in GMD–CCP alliance, and lucky to escape massacre, 1927. Later aided Nanchang Uprising. 1931, joined  Mao. Survived Long March, became firm supporter of Mao. 1949 prime minister and principal spokesman on foreign affairs. His skill and sense won wide respect abroad and in China.

Zhu De, 1886–1976. Born in Sichuan. Athletics teacher, then army officer. Went first to France and then Germany, became friend of Zhou Enlai and communist. 1927, led uprising at Nanchang against GMD, which failed. 1928, joined Mao. C-in-  C of Red Army until retirement in 1954. Always closely involved with his soldiers and their behaviour.

4 The Long March

Breaking out

The blockade of the Jiangxi base was alarmingly effective, and in September 1934 the CCP made plans to withdraw. The decision to abandon their soviet must have been difficult, especially for Mao who was just recovering from malaria. But one more determined GMD campaign might destroy them altogether.

On the night of 15 October there began the retreat which developed into the heroic Long March. According to most reports their official number was about 100,000, being some 85,000 soldiers and 15,000 other communists, with only 35 women members. An engineer of the Red Army Arsenal subsequently described their departure to American journalist Agnes Smedley:

'Each man carried five pounds of ration rice, and each had a shoulder pole from which hung either two small boxes of ammunition or hand grenades, or big kerosene cans filled with our most essential machinery and tools. Each pack contained a blanket or quilt, one quilted winter uniform and three pairs of strong cloth shoes with thick rope soles . . . Each man had a drinking cup, a pair of chopsticks thrust into his puttees and a needle and thread caught on the underside of the peak of his cap. All men wore big sun-rain hats made of two thin layers of bamboo with oiled paper between, and many had paper umbrellas stuck into their packs. Each man carried a rifle.'

Leaving bands of partisans behind to conceal their withdrawal, they moved by night and reached the third line of encirclement before the GMD realised they had gone.

The commander-in-chief of the Red Army was Zhu De, with Peng Dehuai as his deputy. The vanguard took the brunt of much of the fighting when that occurred. It was led by Lin Biao, later one of Mao's closest associates. Zhou Enlai, as political commissar, travelled in the centre of the column with the Headquarters Unit, which also included Mao Zedong with his second wife, Ho Zichen, and his brother Zemin. Then came the Supply Section, the Arsenal, the medical orderlies and – not least in importance – the Drama Unit, which won the support of illiterate peasants along the way by giving propagandist entertainment.

None of the early marchers could have imagined how far and how arduous the trek was to become. Referred to generally in China as 'The 25,000-*li* March', its route included many reversals and detours, and is estimated to have been at least 18,100 *li* or 9,660 km (6,000 miles). Many had to march further. Of those who began it, fewer than one in three completed the journey safely.

They had neither adequate maps nor a precisely planned route. At first they had intended to head northwest, towards another soviet already established in Sichuan. But they faced a heavy GMD attack when crossing the Xiang River, and decided instead to cling to the mountains and move further west. This course took them through a part of Guangxi where live the Miaos, one of about fifty 'minority peoples' who together make up seven per cent of China's population.

With the support of the Miaos the Red Army crossed into Guizhou. There it was helped on its way by local peasants, and by supplies captured from warehouses belonging to wealthy landlords.

Zunyi

By clever strategy based on Mao's recollection of an episode from *Romance of Three Kingdoms*, the Red Army seized the city of Zunyi. There the marchers paused to reorganise and discuss future plans. At a most important conference in January 1935, Mao finally won his argument against continued obedience to Moscow's Comintern. But for several years Moscow ignored the significance of that decision.

A modern Chinese painting celebrates Mao's victory at Loushan Pass. The pass, near the city of Zunyi, was a forbidding challenge to the Red Army. Mao's poem about it ends:
'Do not say the strong pass is guarded with iron.
This very day with firm step we shall cross its summit
We shall cross its summit!
Here the hills are blue like the sea
And the dying sun is like blood.'
And cross the summit they did, but they had to contend with even more difficult terrain later in the march.

At Zunyi Mao was elected Chairman of the CCP, an office he kept for the rest of his life. Most of the other Party leaders, including Zhou Enlai, now accepted absolutely his tactics of reliance on guerrilla warfare and peasant support. As the official purpose of the March they adopted the slogan 'Go north and fight the Japanese'. One member who withdrew from the march here was the Chairman of the Labour Federation, Liu Shaoqi, with whom Mao was to clash a few decades later.

While the communists paused at Zunyi, Chiang Kai-shek reinforced the GMD defence of all possible crossing-places on the great Changjiang River. The Red Army's hopes of moving north were again frustrated. Instead, over the next few weeks the communists confused their enemy by rapid deceptive moves and speedy changes of direction. Late in February they captured the formidable Loushan Pass. Two days later they returned to take Zunyi a second time. In all this fighting their destruction of twenty GMD regiments marked the first Red victory of the March. It provoked Chiang to disregard the Japanese threat. He moved more GMD troops into the Zunyi area; by April the Red Army was compelled to go still further south, and then west to the difficult gorges of Yunnan.

There, while a diversion by the vanguard distracted GMD attention and also won valuable medical supplies, the main army seized the ferry crossing on the Jinsha River, the swift and turbulent upper stream of the Changjiang. Despite recruitment of some 20,000 volunteers since the March had begun, its numbers were now only about 65,000. All, including the vanguard, safely crossed the Jinsha.

Crossing the Dadu

At last the Red Army was able to head north, but the route lay through forbidding forests and fearsome mountain passes. Fortunately for them the communists gained the friendship of the local minority peoples, the Yi and Lolo tribes. The Lolo chieftain and his escort conducted them through this wild territory as far as the roaring Dadu River, which races down from Tibetan peaks to form a major tributary of the Changjiang.

The crossing of the Dadu is often mentioned as the supreme example of heroism in the whole epic journey. The vanguard captured the ferry and crossed successfully. But the GMD defenders promptly called up aircraft by radio, and the main body of the marchers got there to find the area being heavily bombed. With its main force stranded on one bank and the vanguard on the other, the Red Army was in deadly danger. Silently and swiftly, marching almost without pause the army pushed its hazardous way to the village of Luding,

about 160 kilometres (100 miles) upstream.

At Luding, where the gorge is deeper and the current stronger, the chains of a suspension bridge spanned the torrent. But for some distance from the bank, the communists found the flooring of the bridge destroyed. While the vanguard harassed the GMD garrison on the far shore, men of the main force felled trees. In spite of being snipers' targets, volunteers swung out high above the river to lay a fresh timber track across the chains. As soon as the gap was filled they began to cross, but then the defenders set fire to the planking at the other end. Fighting their way through the flames, several of the attackers were shot down and fell into the torrent far below. But a final rush swept the GMD defenders aside. The triumph at the Luding bridge became an inspiration to others faced by seemingly impossible odds.

Months of hardship

Further trials were yet to come. It took the Red Army seven weeks to cover the next hundred miles, climbing the permanent snows and glaciers of the Tibetan border region. Few tracks existed, and where they did they were treacherous. Each man had to carry his own arms plus enough food and fuel to last him ten days. Instead of their usual rice they now had to eat boiled wheat, which caused many to become ill, while the high altitude and extreme cold made breathing difficult and speech more so. The Medical Unit moved to the rear to assist the exhausted, one of whom was Mao's wife, wounded in the earlier fighting. But Zhu De's wife continued to carry her own rifle and knapsack, and sometimes even to help others. Mao himself developed a serious fever and was transported on a stretcher. Now more than ever the unswerving loyalty and good sense of Zhu De upheld the morale and welfare of the remaining 45,000.

In June, when these survivors were utterly weary, they were joined by 50,000 quite fit troops from the soviet formed in Sichuan, relatively nearby. The Sichuan leader, Zhang Guotao, posed the first real challenge to Mao's position and authority within the CCP. While everyone rested and recov-

ered, Party meetings firmly endorsed Mao's Chairmanship, and issued a long 'Appeal to Fellow Countrymen concerning Resistance to Japan'. Then Mao set off northwards again with half the Army, leaving Zhu De behind with the resentful Zhang.

This terrible section of their journey took the heaviest toll of lives. It involved crossing the dreaded Grasslands, a vast eerie bog, mist-shrouded and bleak, devoid of life and swept frequently by hail or sleet. Daily the marchers staggered through coarse, tall grass growing in smelly black mud; by

Crossing the Great Snow Mountains, another heroic episode on the Long March. Remember that these modern artists are illustrating a legend, and perhaps at the time there were no heroic poses, only weary, battered men struggling with a desperate situation.

night they had to sleep standing up, leaning back to back, and always carrying their armaments and food supplies.

When eventually the communists reached firm ground, the GMD forces waiting for them were so demoralised by their own poor conditions and so impressed by the Red Army's fortitude that many changed sides. Together they pressed on over Mount Liupan and into North Shaanxi. There, for Mao and his comrades, the ordeal of the Long March ended on 20 October 1935. A year later they were joined by those who had stayed with Zhu De, and by communists from other parts of China.

Mao's determination to establish a major base in Shaanxi was prompted by his concern for defence of China against the threat of Japanese invasion. This would attract more popular support, and serve to educate the public towards a more communal outlook. Yanan, which soon became the centre of communist government, was ideal as a base. The CCP could give a lead to all patriotic Chinese and build up forces within range of the region occupied by the Japanese. From the danger areas refugees, including technicians and

artisans, students and professors, flocked to Yanan. There, in what rapidly became a crowded city, they lived in caves dug into the soft sandstone hillsides.

Mao too lived in such a cave. His partisan wife, Ho Zichen, worn out by her experiences, had gone to Moscow for treatment and their marriage was annulled. In the quiet of the Yanan nights he wrote many poems and essays exalting those who had died during the March, reaffirming his belief in their ideals and declaring his confidence in the ordinary people.

The Long March began as a retreat from GMD blockade in southeast China. Its survivors achieved success in northwest China. On the way they won lasting friendship from peasants and from minority peoples. Unlike previous armies throughout China's history, the communists always paid for anything taken from the poor. At the same time, performances by propaganda teams of the Drama Unit explained their viewpoint to the villagers. Above all, the heroism of the Red Army soldiers throughout the prolonged ordeal won a new respect for their sincerity and enthusiasm not merely from the common folk but from almost all classes.

For Mao, the March marked the triumph of his policies as distinct from those of Russia, and it brought confirmation of his leadership of the Chinese Communist Party.

1934, October The Long March began from Jiangxi.

1935, January Zunyi Conference accepted Mao's leadership of Chinese communism.

1935, May Crossing of the Luding Bridge over the Dadu River.

1935, October Mao's army reached Shaanxi.

Below: *Always Mao wanted CCP officials to enjoy friendly understanding with the ordinary people. Here he chats happily with manual workers.*

Above: *In his Yanan cave house, Mao did a great deal of writing, including his article 'On Protracted War' in which he said:*

> *'All wars that are progressive are just and all wars that impede progress are unjust. We communists oppose all unjust wars that impede progress, but we do not oppose progressive, just wars.'*

Clearly at this time he viewed the GMD assaults against the CCP as an unjust impediment to progress, but war against Japanese invaders as being justifiable. However, in another article composed in his Yanan cave just six months later he wrote:

> *'Every communist must grasp the truth, "Political power grows out of the barrel of a gun."'*

21

5 Wars and their consequences

The united front against Japan

In Shaanxi, south of Yanan, is the ancient city of Xian. Based at Xian and nominally attached to the GMD were the Manchurian troops who had escaped when Japan occupied their homeland. In 1936 these troops agreed with Zhou Enlai and Mao to co-operate fully against further Japanese incursions. Consequently in December, when Chiang Kai-shek visited Xian, urging them to attack the Yanan base, the Manchurians kidnapped and held him until, unwillingly, he consented to a new United Front.

Agreement was reached by which the GMD undertook to stop its persecution of the CCP. For its part the CCP accepted the Guomindang government at Nanjing. The Red Army was renamed as the Eighth Route Army of Chiang's national command. Both sides agreed that the republic should be based upon Sun Yat-sen's Three Principles of the People, but they ignored the different interpretations of those principles.

Many CCP members were reluctant to co-operate with the GMD. They remembered Chiang's betrayal in 1927, the extermination campaigns against the Jiangxi soviet, the hardships of the Long March. But Mao reminded them that,

as decided at Zunyi, their first task must be resistance to Japan. As Mao hoped, many non-communists were favourably impressed by his apparent willingness to place national defence before political quarrels. To gain yet wider support the communists dropped their former policy of seizing land for the peasants. They called instead for fair but strict rent control, which was less likely to upset landlords.

The Yanan settlement prospered. The army helped in the development of industry and agriculture. Schools and a university were set up.

In July 1937, the Japanese army, which had long occupied much of northern China, held an exercise near Beijing. It provoked a local skirmish which rapidly developed into full-scale war. By the end of the month the GMD abandoned Beijing to avoid its possible destruction. In August Japan opened a second front, against Shanghai, China's great financial centre, and Chiang Kai-shek stubbornly ordered his best troops to hold their positions there at all costs. Despite heavy losses against superior air and naval forces the defence held on for nearly three months. Then the enemy bypassed it to attack Nanjing, which fell in December. With Nanjing, Shanghai too was lost.

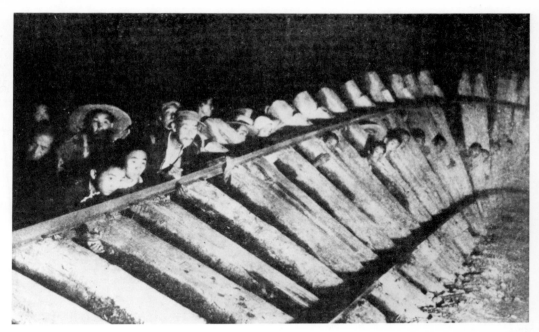

left: *Japanese air-raids against Shanghai and Nanjing in 1937 caused great devastation. In Manchuria a few years earlier Japan shocked the world by being the first nation to bomb civilian areas indiscriminately. She continued to do so, attacking China's crowded cities.*

right: *Sabotage was carried out by patriotic groups organised by the communist bases set up in rural areas between the Japanese-held cities.*

With the fall of Nanjing the government capital was moved up the Changjiang River to Wuhan. GMD troops fought valiantly but unsuccessfully to halt the Japanese advance, which now spread in a pincer movement to north and south of the Changjiang. In June, 1938, Chiang Kai-shek ordered the breaching of the dykes of the Huanghe River. The flooding of towns and farmlands hampered the enemy, but the scale of the disaster to the people of the region caused many to fear Chiang as a callous dictator. The standing of the GMD fell further with the loss of Guangzhou in October, and then of Wuhan itself in December, 1938.

Wartime disagreements

As the Japanese advanced, the communists in Shaanxi moved against their northern front. In September 1937, Zhu De's Eighth Route Army had scored the first victory, capturing large quantities of ammunition and supplies. Behind the Japanese advance communist guerrilla bases were set up from which to conduct surprise raids and sabotage. CCP members made sure that fair and considerate treatment was given to all local people so long as they supported such activities, whether for patriotic or political reasons. A major guerrilla force, called the New Fourth Army and linked with Yanan by secret radio, was established in the lower Changjiang region.

From Wuhan, Chiang Kai-shek moved his capital far up the river to Chongqing in Sichuan. Relatively secure from attack here, he adopted the maxim 'use space to buy time'. and awaited Japan's eventual defeat by other powers. But Chiang was suspicious of the communists. He feared they would use their guerrilla organisation to convert people to their cause. He used GMD troops not so much to fight the Japanese as to disrupt the CCP's influence, and he ordered a blockade of Yanan. Chiang was especially worried by the existence of the New Fourth Army so near his own former capital and, in January 1941, he arranged its destruction by GMD forces. Thus the second United Front ended.

Chiang's attitude rebounded against him. He refused to allow the arming of civilians against the invader because he feared it might be difficult to control them after the war. Meanwhile his army, with no real purpose, lost heart and discipline. His government's retreat to Chongqing deprived it of revenue from the wealthier coastal provinces, where the

Key events	1936	Xian Incident: kidnapping of Chiang Kai-shek led to second United Front, against Japan.
	1937	War against Japan, and speedy Japanese advance.
	1941	Breakdown of United Front as CCP and GMD troops clash.
	1945	Surrender of Japan.

industrial and commercial cities were now occupied by the Japanese and the rural areas by communist-organised sabotage groups. Without revenue the GMD government attempted no social or economic reforms. Instead it printed quantities of paper money. The result was inflation, and that led to widespread corruption, administrative inefficiency and the financial ruin of many of the GMD's middle-class supporters.

The last civil war

Increasingly, Chinese of all classes grew to respect the CCP as leaders of the only real resistance against a foreign enemy. The Yanan region under blockade became more self-reliant. Refugees continued to flock to it, and a local militia of farmer–soldiers was formed. The effects of inflation were overcome by sharing out goods equally and avoiding the use of money. Officials were seen to do their fair share of work in co-operative enterprises. Mao made sure that administration worked fairly and smoothly, and that newcomers fitted easily into the community. He advocated what he termed 'New Democracy', which differed from the Russian model by requiring election of representatives to local committees from each social class.

By 1945, as well as the Yanan area, the CCP controlled nineteen separate 'liberated' areas, each administered as a 'New Democracy'. Consequently many people in China came to recognise Mao's authority and to respect the nature of his government. However, except for a few intrepid foreign correspondents such as Edgar Snow and Agnes Smedley, the Western world communicated only with Chongqing, and therefore continued to regard the nationalist GMD as the popular and dominant government of China.

above: *Volunteer guerrilla fighters were trained in increasing numbers by the CCP. Until more weapons were captured in raids against the Japanese, they had to train with makeshift weapons, because the GMD did not favour issuing arms to everybody.*

below: *Mao moves from battle to battle, northern Shaanxi, 1947.*

Accordingly, when Japan was defeated in the Pacific, America helped Chiang by airlifting GMD troops to take over the northern and eastern cities. To many Chinese, this move looked like biased interference. But the CCP, slighted by the Americans, retained control over the rural areas between the cities. Conferences arranged by the Americans produced an agreement to a coalition government; but like previous attempts at GMD–CCP unity this failed, and the two parties soon became embroiled again in civil war. Perhaps Mao would have preferred to gain domination over the whole country more securely by the slower means of political persuasion; but once war was unavoidable he maintained that determination and honest leadership must triumph over corruption and selfishness.

The civil war lasted for three years. By 1949 Mao's confidence was justified. Though at first larger and better armed, the GMD forces lacked the spirit and determination of the Red Army – now renamed the People's Liberation Army, or PLA. Chiang Kai-shek spread his armies far and wide in an attempt to hold all northern China. But, finding themselves attacked from all sides and distrusting their own leaders, the nationalist troops often gave up their arms or went over to the PLA. By 1948 Chiang's forces were in retreat. Beijing surrendered to Lin Biao in January 1949, and throughout that year Zhu De and Peng Dehuai respectively won the provinces to the south and west. Chiang and his remaining followers sought refuge on the island of Taiwan.

The People's Republic

The People's Republic of China was proclaimed in Beijing by Mao Zedong on 1 October 1949.

He announced that it would be based on an alliance of workers and peasants. Though at first it would be controlled largely by military or police forces, Mao preferred benevolent persuasion to force. The great majority of the people, wearied by many years of war and insecurity, greeted their new government with hope. Some foreign powers, too, accepted the new regime; Britain did, but the USA did not. In February 1950 the new regime signed a Treaty of Friendship with Russia, which would provide technical assistance in urgently needed reconstruction and rehabilitation. The railways and canal system were quickly restored and used to

Mao proclaims the People's Republic in Beijing, 1949.

distribute food and fuel to people impoverished by war. All were treated equally and fairly; and the PLA took a lead in work for peaceful development.

One of Mao's first steps was a new Marriage Law, granting women's rights and freedom of choice. Land reform, his other urgent concern, was introduced in June 1950. All cultivated land was to be redistributed equally among the peasants. Landlords were to have the same share as others so that they could work on it themselves and learn a reformed way of life through manual labour.

But in that month war broke out within the neighbouring country of Korea. At first this was no concern of China's, but it caused an alarmed America to interfere, fearing the spread of communism. America's move to defend the straits of Taiwan was seen as support for the defeated Chiang Kai-shek. Worse, American and United Nations participation on the side of South Korea threatened China's northern industrial area. Despite warnings from Zhou Enlai in Beijing and the US President in Washington, the American-led forces

Key events

1938	New Democracy Movement: Mao planned a new form of communist rule to bring together all classes.
1946–9	Civil war (or 'War of Liberation') ending in communist victory.
1949	People's Republic of China proclaimed by Mao.
1950	Land Reform distributed land among the peasants.
1950–3	Korean War: China and N. Korea against USA, the United Nations and S. Korea.
1952	Five-Anti Campaign, aiming to clean up corruption.

advanced towards the Chinese border. The CCP reacted by dramatically changing its intended programme. Hundreds of thousands of Chinese crossed into Korea under the command of Peng Dehuai, and the war there raged on until 1953. Among those killed in action was Mao's son, Anying.

The war forced Mao to hold back some reforms and speed up others. Tighter controls replaced the earlier moderate policies. Major industries and businesses were nationalised, along with all labour relations, hospitals and schools, thus ending all Western or capitalist influence in the economy. Since China and its new government seemed threatened by outsiders, such sweeping measures gained more popular support than they might otherwise have done.

The CCP had achieved economic and political stability. The Party went on to launch its 'Five-Anti Campaign', against all those suspected of corruption and hoarding. Merchants and businessmen accused of dishonesty, bribery or fraud were fined heavily. Some were executed, but many survived because they promised loyalty, and the government wished to use their skills. They were allowed to keep a share of profit in return for their co-operation.

The Five-Anti Campaign spread to the countryside. Here, beyond the reach of government control, millions more were killed as a result of long-standing hatreds and the vengeance of a previously oppressed people. There are no reliable figures for the deaths in these official and unofficial purges, but the total certainly was high. Such a slaughter cannot be excused. But it should be remembered that millions had died

from starvation in pre-communist China, and that as a result of these upheavals the land once held by four million landlords was shared among some three hundred million peasants.

Late in 1954, after five years as Chairman of the People's Republic, Mao might have summed up his government's record like this:

They had failed to gain Taiwan, the last remnant of China, because of the Korean War.

They had not gained admission to the United Nations or complete acceptance as a world power because of American opposition.

But they had a balanced budget and economic stability.

They had encouraged mining and industry.

They had destroyed the old order in the countryside; the landlords were gone and there was a chance to build a new rural society and economy.

They were helping the new peasant landholders to cooperate; and improving production by means of irrigation projects and pest control.

They were busily teaching the masses to read and write; and through constant slogans and propaganda had much improved health and hygiene.

But Mao was not yet satisfied with his revolutionary progress.

6 Recurrent revolution

Key events	1953–8	First Five-Year Plan to develop industry and agriculture.
	1955	Mao called for more village farming collectives.
	1956	Hundred Flowers Movement: Mao asked for advice and criticism.
	1958	Great Leap Forward: Mao demanded rapid economic growth and formation of large agricultural communes. Dazhai Commune in Shanxi, though a poor community, made a great success of terracing and irrigation. In 1964 Mao told all Chinese, 'In agriculture, learn from Dazhai.'

'Hundred Flowers' and 'Great Leap Forward'

Giving land to the peasants meant that many millions of farmers had only tiny plots of land. In 1955 Mao led the way in encouraging the peasants of each village to form co-operatives, to give up their separate holdings and work together. Yields were shared according to work done.

In the towns too Mao wished to see socialism grow, so that all would work and share together. But he feared that this might produce nothing but bureaucracy: there would be too many regulations and officials who did nothing useful. Here lay the roots of conflict between Mao and many of the other CCP leaders, including his deputy Liu Shaoqi and Liu's ally, Deng Xiaoping. They sought to plan and organise from the centre. The first Five-Year Plan to increase China's output in industry and agriculture started in 1953. But Mao soon became impatient. He had great faith in the ordinary workers, and he suspected that the planners might simply become new bosses, as corrupt and selfish as the officials of former times. In 1956 he invited suggestions from scholars and writers for improving the communist system of doing things, saying 'Let a hundred flowers blossom, let a hundred schools of thought contend.'

Encouraged by this, critics of the government became increasingly outspoken. Generally Mao agreed with what they said about bureaucratic officials and thoughtless copying of Russian ideas. But many CCP officials naturally objected, for they were only trying to do their duty. By 1957 they were calling their critics 'poisonous weeds' rather than 'flowers'.

Mao apparently accepted this attitude. The 'Hundred Flowers' campaign was swiftly dropped, and those who criticised the government were punished. This ended any real hope of freedom of thought in China, and reinforced the dictatorial power of the Party.

But the next year, in 1958, Mao launched another new

Peasants of a commune, following the Dazhai spirit of self-reliance, terrace their slopes for growing rice with irrigation from mountain streams.

drive. He wanted to reduce the reliance on Russia, and announced the 'Great Leap Forward'. He believed that mass enthusiasm rather than material rewards could inspire efforts towards higher production. He urged merging the village co-operatives into huge communes of up to 50,000 people each. These swiftly came into being, organised in 'production

The People's Liberation Army was expected to work with the peasants. Here some are helping with the harvest. But this is during the Cultural Revolution, and they have paused to study Chairman Mao's works.

development of communes helped to overcome these gaps by moving many city people to help in the country, and forming large mixed groups to work on building and irrigation projects. The energies of all involved in these great efforts built up enthusiastic activity and strengthened the bonds between Mao and the people.

But again things went wrong. Some of the experiments in rural industry were completely impracticable and failed dismally. Over-enthusiasm led some communes to exaggerate their output. These mistakes upset some of the officials in Beijing, who were worried that the communes were gaining greater independence in running things themselves.

Weary of hostility within the Party and of political dispute, Mao gave up being head of government in December, 1958. But he remained Chairman of the CCP. The new Chairman of the People's Republic was Liu Shaoqi.

Mao under attack

One of the most outspoken critics of what Mao had tried to do was the defence minister, Peng Dehuai. On a visit to Moscow in 1959 Peng blamed Mao for the increasing disagreements between China and Russia, and described the Great Leap Forward as a disaster. He also upset Mao by putting professional officers and a rank system into the army. Mao demanded that Peng be dismissed and replaced by his own close friend, Lin Biao. As a result the split with Russia worsened, and in 1960 Moscow withdrew all its aid and advisers, demanding repayment of all its loans.

In 1960 and 1961 China suffered typhoons, floods and droughts, causing food shortage, transport problems and widespread starvation. The new communes faced great difficulties, though they eventually achieved success. Mao largely kept out of the political arena. Thus Liu was free to control the economy in his own way. Liu believed that Mao's reliance on mass enthusiasm had weakened government authority. He wanted more power to guide industry, and he relied on material rewards to encourage production even though this brought social inequality.

Mao thought Liu was working against the original ideals of the revolution. Through Lin Biao he was able to control the army, which was devoted to his revolutionary ideas. But he feared that Liu, with the CCP general secretary, Deng

brigades' and 'mutual aid teams'. Each commune chose its own leaders, and with guidance from CCP members they planned the production work for everyone, including the women, who were expected to play a full part. The communes built up small industries, steel furnaces and workshops to supply their own needs. Each had canteens, schools and hospitals to serve its members.

Mao always hated distinctions between town and country dwellers, between mental and manual workers. The swift

Key people

Liu Shaoqi, 1898–1969. Like Mao came from Hunan. As a communist thinker and writer he was second to Mao from 1930s on. In 1959 he succeeded Mao as Chairman of the People's Republic. His policies called for increased central party control,
and for material rewards as incentives. Overthrown and disgraced in the Cultural Revolution, he died in prison. In 1980 his good reputation was officially restored.

Peng Dehuai, 1898–1974. Came from a wealthy peasant family in Hunan. Led a mutiny against the GMD in 1928, and joined Mao in Jiangxi. Helped build up the Red Army, and commanded Chinese forces in Korea, 1950–3. Defence minister,
1954–9. Pro-Russian, he publicly criticised Mao's policies, so was dismissed and disgraced. After Mao's death his good reputation was officially restored.

Lin Biao, 1907–71. Became a close friend of Mao during the Long March. A successful general in the war against Japan and civil war. In 1959 defence minister, reformed and democratised the army. Compiled the 'Little Red Book' of Mao's
Thoughts. In 1969 became Mao's official heir, but killed in an air crash while apparently plotting against Mao.

Deng Xiaoping, 1904– . Educated in France and Russia, an early member of the CCP. He was on the Long March, and in the army during the Anti-Japanese war and civil war. In 1956 general secretary of the CCP, and a close associate of Liu Shaoqi.
Dismissed in Cultural Revolution, reinstated and acted as prime minister, 1974–6. Disgraced again after death of Zhou Enlai, but returned to power after Mao's death. His policies included closer friendship with Western powers, destruction of the radical 'Gang of Four', modernisation of Chinese agriculture, technology and defence, permitting social inequalities with limited freedom of speech. He claimed to be Marxist and Maoist, but was celebrated for his remark, 'It doesn't matter if a cat is black or white as long as it catches mice.'

Jiang Qing, 1914– . Mao's last wife, was an actress who met him in Yanan. During the Cultural Revolution she imposed tight controls on the arts, banning Western influence and Chinese tradition in the theatre. After Mao's
death she and her colleagues (the 'Gang of Four') were imprisoned by Mao's successors, who feared her ambitions.

Key events		
	1960	Disagreements growing sharper between China and Russia: Russia withdrew all aid.
	1966–9	Cultural Revolution. Removal of Mao's opponents in the CCP, and of 'bureaucratic' officials. The Red Guards, waving Mao's *Thoughts*, attacked institutions and individuals.
	1976	Deaths of Zhou Enlai, Zhu De and Mao Zedong.

Xiaoping, was using the schools and newspapers to guide people away from Mao's own views on freedom and equality. Government officials were once again coming to regard themselves as superior to other people. Mao determined on a new struggle. His determination became the Cultural Revolution.

Cultural Revolution

A large poster appeared at Beijing University in May, 1966, urging students to rebel against repression by the authorities. Large numbers responded. In July Mao showed his fitness to lead a new movement of young enthusiasts: he swam four-teen kilometres (nine miles) across the Changjiang River in a blaze of publicity. He told the young people they needed to experience the same kind of struggle that his own generation had gone through, that they needed to make a new revolution. In August he displayed his own large poster, 'Bombard the Headquarters'.

In the Cultural Revolution an army of students called Red Guards waved copies of the 'Little Red Book' and, urged on by posters, rebelled against those officials accused of wielding authority unfairly.

Thousands of dissatisfied students, the 'Red Guards', became the forefront of Mao's new revolution. Lin Biao had compiled a 'Little Red Book' of Mao's writings for the army; now each Red Guard carried a copy, and set out to destroy all whom they claimed opposed its ideas.

The Red Guards' first target was Liu Shaoqi, who was removed from office in November 1966, and Sun Yat-sen's widow acted as head of government for the next few years. Then they went on to attack other leaders and officials. They demanded sweeping changes in schools, theatres and industry to remove anything that seemed out-of-date or denied social equality. They became increasingly destructive. They split into factions, and when they were joined by radical apprentices from Shanghai workshops they became even more violent. Mao's wife Jiang Qing, a former actress, made herself responsible for cultural matters. She and her supporters went far beyond Mao's own intentions for the revolutionary shake-up.

The turmoil continued until 1969 before order was restored. Mao had won back undisputed power, though the country had been brought near to civil war. He promptly used his new strength to build up the rural communes, particularly in health care and agricultural production. His opponents, such as Peng and Liu and Deng Xiaoping, were disgraced; while his friend, Lin Biao, enjoyed great popularity and in 1969 was officially named to succeed Mao. Through all the changes Mao's ally Zhou Enlai remained prime minister; his skill and moderation helped to preserve China from the worst dangers of upheaval.

Once again after the Cultural Revolution it was necessary to restore effective government. Some of the Party officials who had been removed were brought back. Lin Biao, who had gained so much personal power from the Cultural Revolution, let it be known that he was distressed by this reversal. Also he disliked the moves begun by Zhou Enlai towards peaceful relations with America. Disagreement

Following the Cultural Revolution education and health services to rural areas were much improved. This girl was nominated by her local community to train as a 'barefoot doctor'; now she treats their common ailments, gives preventive medicines and refers serious cases to hospital.

arose between Mao and Lin Biao over these matters.

In September 1971 Lin was suspected of plotting to take over power from the ageing Mao, and he fled in an aeroplane. It crashed on the way to the Russian border, killing Lin himself and those with him.

Mao's last revolution had ended in confusion and uncertainty. Now nearing eighty, Mao still relied on the friendship of his aged comrades, Zhu De and Zhou Enlai. Each of them was ill. Mao realised that his lifelong ideals were not yet fully accomplished and perhaps never could be; and he lamented that the Cultural Revolution had failed to produce a successor to continue his struggle. In 1975 in a poem dedicated to Zhou he wrote:

'Loyal parents who sacrificed so much for the nation never feared the ultimate fate.
Now that the country has become Red, who will be its guardians?
Our mission, unfinished, may take a thousand years.
The struggle tires us and our hair is grey.
You and I, old friend, can we just watch our efforts being washed away?'

Zhou Enlai died in January 1976, and Zhu De in July. During his last months of illness Mao named Hua Guofeng as his successor to limit the danger of false claimants or bloody intrigues after his death. He died on 9 September 1976.

China after Mao

Soon after Mao's death his widow, Jiang Qing, and her close supporters were imprisoned as political extremists seeking personal power. Denounced as 'The Gang of Four', they were brought to trial four years later. Meanwhile, though Hua Guofeng remained nominal Chairman until 1981, the survivors of those overthrown by the Cultural Revolution held effective power. Led by Deng Xiaoping, they restored official respect for those previously disgraced and reversed Mao's more idealistic policies.

Born in poverty and obscurity during the decay of China's last imperial dynasty, Mao Zedong achieved world stature as one of the most influential leaders of this century. Within China he was also acclaimed as a poet and writer.

He rejected the Russian pattern of communism and persisted with the development of his own interpretation of that creed. When the CCP, which he helped to found, seemed fated to expire, he became its Chairman and led it to eventual victory.

The China whose government Mao and the CCP undertook in 1949 was exhausted after many decades of corruption, exploitation, poverty and wars. By the time of Mao's death in 1976 the entire population of his People's Republic enjoyed sufficient food, an enviable system of health care, a steadily rising standard of living and a stable economy; the Chinese nation was a recognised member of the United Nations, its agricultural development earned international admiration and its industrial production was the sixth highest in the world.

Though the last decade of Mao's life was chaotic, with its sudden changes, violence and controversy, few would deny that the overall achievements of his long lifetime were truly remarkable.

Chinese names

	Chinese Characters		Older spelling	New spelling
Personal names	陳 獨 秀	1879–1942	Ch'en Tu-hsiu	Chen Duxiu
	慈 禧	1835–1908	Tz'u Hsi	Ci Xi
	鄧 小 平	1904–	Teng Hsiao-p'ing	Deng Xiaoping
	华 国 鋒	1920–	Hua Kuo-feng	Hua Guofeng
	江 青	1914–	Chiang Ch'ing	Jiang Qing
	康 有 為	1858–1927	K'ang Yu-wei	Kang Youwei
	林 彪	1907–1971	Lin Piao	Lin Biao
	劉 少 奇	1898–1969	Liu Shao-ch'i	Liu Shaoqi
	毛 沢 東	1893–1976	Mao Tse-tung	Mao Zedong
	彭 德 懷	1898–1974	P'eng Teh-huai	Peng Dehuai
	汪 精 衛	1883–1944	Wang Ching-wei	Wang Jingwei
	袁 世 凱	1859–1916	Yüan Shih-k'ai	Yuan Shikai
	張 国 燾	1897–	Chang Kuo-t'ao	Zhang Guotao
	周 恩 來	1898–1976	Chou En-lai	Zhou Enlai
	朱 德	1886–1976	Chu Teh	Zhu De
	蔣 介 石	1887–1975	Chiang Kai-shek	
	孫 逸 仙	1866–1925	Sun Yat-sen	

} These two names retain their earlier spelling because they are in provincial dialects and modern transliteration of the characters would change the pronunciation.

	Former name	New name		Former name	New name
Provinces	Kwangsi	Guangxi	**Cities and towns**	Peking	Beijing
	Kweichow	Guizhou		Chungking	Chongqing
	Kiangsi	Jiangxi		Canton	Guangzhou
	Shensi	Shaanxi		Luting	Luding
	Shantung	Shandong		Nanch'ang	Nanchang
	Shansi	Shanxi		Nanking	Nanjing
	Szechuan	Sichuan		Juichin	Ruijin
				Tientsin	Tianjin
Rivers	Yangtse-kiang	Changjiang		Hankow (Wuhan)	Wuhan
	Tatu	Dadu		Sian	Xian
	Yellow River	Huanghe		Hsiang-hsiang	Xiangxiang
	Golden Sands River	Jinsha		Yenan	Yanan
	Hsiang	Xiang		Tsunyi	Zunyi
				Mt Chingkang	Jinggangshan
				Kuomintang (KMT)	Guomindang (GMD)

Index

Acknowledgments

The author and publisher would like to thank the following for permission to reproduce illustrations:

Front cover, pp 19, 21 (bottom), 31 Anglo-Chinese Educational Institute; pp 6, 7 (left) The Mansell Collection; pp 13, 14, 18, 20, 23, 27, 28, 30 *China Reconstructs*; pp 22, 24 (top) BBC Hulton Picture Library

Map by Reg Piggott

Mao moves from battle to battle, northern Shaanxi, 1947.

front cover: *Chairman Mao Zedong is here portrayed during the Cultural Revolution as a wise, benevolent leader. His Red Guard armband shows his sympathy for the young and his belief in the need for lifelong struggle against repressive officialdom.*

back cover: *Chinese stamps depict Chairman Mao and the achievements of the People's Republic as well as reminders of China's ancient culture.*

The Cambridge History Library

The Cambridge Introduction to History
Written by Trevor Cairns

PEOPLE BECOME CIVILIZED

THE ROMANS AND THEIR EMPIRE

BARBARIANS, CHRISTIANS, AND MUSLIMS

THE MIDDLE AGES

EUROPE AROUND THE WORLD

EUROPE AND THE WORLD

THE BIRTH OF MODERN EUROPE

THE OLD REGIME AND THE REVOLUTION

POWER FOR THE PEOPLE

The Cambridge Topic Books
General Editor Trevor Cairns

THE AMERICAN WAR OF INDEPENDENCE

BENIN: AN AFRICAN KINGDOM AND CULTURE

THE BUDDHA

BUILDING THE MEDIEVAL CATHEDRALS

CHINA AND MAO ZEDONG

CHRISTOPHER WREN
AND ST. PAUL'S CATHEDRAL

THE EARLIEST FARMERS AND THE FIRST CITIES

EARLY CHINA AND THE WALL

THE FIRST SHIPS AROUND THE WORLD

GANDHI AND THE STRUGGLE
FOR INDIA'S INDEPENDENCE

HERNAN CORTES: CONQUISTADOR IN MEXICO

HITLER AND THE GERMANS

THE INDUSTRIAL REVOLUTION BEGINS

LIFE IN A FIFTEENTH-CENTURY MONASTERY

LIFE IN A MEDIEVAL VILLAGE

LIFE IN THE IRON AGE

LIFE IN THE OLD STONE AGE

THE MAORIS

MARTIN LUTHER

MEIJI JAPAN

THE MURDER OF ARCHBISHOP THOMAS

MUSLIM SPAIN

THE NAVY THAT BEAT NAPOLEON

THE PARTHENON

POMPEII

THE PYRAMIDS

THE ROMAN ARMY

THE ROMAN ENGINEERS

ST. PATRICK AND IRISH CHRISTIANITY

THE VIKING SHIPS

The Cambridge History Library will be expanded in the future to include additional volumes. Lerner Publications Company is pleased to participate in making this excellent series of books available to a wide audience of readers.

Lerner Publications Company
241 First Avenue North, Minneapolis, Minnesota 55401